5 INSPIRING SPEECHES OF FAMOUS PERSONALITIES

INDEX

MUNIBA MAZARI

WE ALL ARE PERFECTLY IMPERFECT

Thank you so much for all the love, for all the warm. Thank you all for accepting me. Thank you very much. Well, I always start my talk with some disclaimer. And that disclaimer is that I never claimed to be a motivational speaker.

Yes, I do speak. But I feel like a storyteller. Because where ever I go I share a story with everyone. I believe in the power of words. Many people speak before they think. But I know the value of words. Words can make you, break you, they can heal your soul, they can damage you forever.

So, I always try to use positive words in my life. Wherever I go, they call it adversity, I call it opportunity. They call it a weakness, I call it strength. They call me to disable, I call myself differently able.

They see my disability.

I see my ability.

There are some incidents that happened in your life. And those incidents are so strong that they change your DNA. Those incidents and accidents are so strong that they break you physically. They deform your body but they transform your soul. Those incidents break you, deform you but they mold you into the best version of you.

And the same thing happened to me.

And I am going to share what exactly happened to me.

I was 18 years old when I got married. I belong to a very conservative family, a Baloch family. My father wanted me to get married and all I said was if that makes you happy, I will say 'YES'. and of course, it was never a happy marriage.

Just about after 2 years of getting married, about 9 years ago, I met a car accident. Somehow my husband fell asleep and the car fell into the ditch.

He managed to jump out, saved himself. I am happy for him. But I stayed inside the car and I sustain a lot of injuries.

My right arm was fractured, whist was fractured, shoulder bone and collarbone was fractured. And because of the rib cage injury, lungs and liver were badly injured.

I couldn't breathe. I lost urine control. That's why I have to wear the bag where ever I go. But that injuries changed me and my life completely. As a person, my perception towards living my life was the spine injury. My backbone was completely crushed. And I got paralyzed for the rest of my life.

So this accident took place in a far-flung area of Balochistan where there was no first aid, no hospital, no ambulance. I was in the middle of nowhere. Many people came to rescue. They drag me out of the car. While they were dragging me out I got the complete transaction of my spinal cord.

And now there was this debate going on, should we keep it here, she is going to die, or where should we go. There was no ambulance. The was one four wheeler jeep standing in the corner of the street. They said, put her in the back of the jeep and take her to the hospital which is 3 hours away from this place.

And I still remember that bumpy ride. I was all broken. They threw me in the back of the jeep and they rushed me to the hospital. That is where I realized that my half body was paralyzed and half body was fractured. I finally ended up in a hospital where I stayed for two and a half months.

I underwent multiple surgeries. Doctors have put a lot of titanium in my arms and there was a lot of titanium on my back to fix my back.

That's why, In Pakistan, people called me the 'Iron Lady' of Pakistan.

Sometimes I wonder how easy it is for me to describe all this all over again. And somebody has rightly said that when you
share your story and it doesn't make you cry, that means you are healing.

Those two and a half months, in the hospital, were droughtful. I will not make a story just to inspire you. I was on the verge of dis-pare.

One day the doctor came to me, and he said, well I heard that you want to be an artist, but you ended up being a housewife.

I have bad news for you.

You won't be able to paint again because your wrist and arm are so deformed. You won't be able to hold the pen again.

And I stayed quiet.

Next day, the doctor came to me and said, your spine injury is so bad you won't be able to walk again.

I took a deep breath. And I said it's alright.

Again, Next day the doctor came and said, because of your spine injury and your fixation that you have in your back, you won't be able to give birth to a child again.

That day, I was devastated.

I still remember, I ask my mother, why me, and that is where I started to question my existence.

Why am I even alive?

What's the point of living?

I couldn't walk, I couldn't paint, fine.

I cannot be a mother and we have this thing in our head being women that we are incomplete without having children, I am going to be an incomplete woman for the rest of my life.

What's the point?

People are scared that they think I will get divorced.

What is going to happen to me?

Why me?

Why Am I alive?

We all try to chase this tunnel.

We all do this.

Because we see lights at the end of the tunnel which keeps us going. My dear friends, in my situation, there was a tunnel that I had to roll on but there was no light.

And that is where I realized the words have the power to heal the soul.

My mother said to me that this two shall-pass. God has a greater plan for you. I don't know what it is. But he surely has.

And all in that distress and grief, mom's those words were so magical that they kept me going. I was trying to put my smile on my face all the time hiding the pain.

It was so hard to hide the pain which was there. But all I knew was that I will give up, my mother and brother will give up too. I cannot see them crying with me.

So what kept me going was one day I asked my brother, I know, I have a deformed hand but I am tired of looking at these white walls in the hospital and wearing this white scraps.

I am getting tired of this.

I want to add more colors to my life.

I want to do something.

Bring me some colors, I want to paint.

so the very first painting I made was on my deathbed. It was not just an art piece or not just my passion.

It was my therapy.

What an amazing therapy it was. without saying a single word, I could paint my heart out. I could share my story. People used to come and say, 'wow, what a lovely painting'. so much color, nobody sees the grief in it.

Only I could.

So that's how I spend my two and a half months in the hospital. Lying, never complaining or whining but painting. And then I was discharged.

And I went back home and I realized that I have developed a lot of pressure ulcers on my back, on my hipbone. I was unable to sit. There were a lot of infections all over my body, a lot of allergies.

So Doctor wanted me to lie down on the bed straight.For not six months, for not 1 year, but for two years I was bedridden confined in that one room looking outside the window listening to the birds chirping and thinking there will be a time when we will be going out with the family and enjoying the nature.

That was the time, where I realized how lucky people are but they don't realize.That is the time where I realized, the day I going to sit, I am going to share this pain to make them realize how blessed they are and they even don't consider them lucky.There are always turning points in your life.

There was a re-birthday that I celebrated.

After two years and two and a half months when I was able to sit in a wheelchair. That was the day where I had the rebirth. I was a completely different person. I still remember the day I sat on the wheelchair first time knowing that I am never going to live this, knowing that I am never going to walk for the rest of my life.

I saw myself in the mirror. and I talked to my self and I still remember what I said.

I cannot wait for a miracle to come and make me walk.

I cannot sit in the corner of the room crying, cripping and begging mercy because nobody has time.

So, I have to accept my self, the way I am, the sooner the better.

So, I applied the lip color for the first time. And I erased it. and I cried and I said what am I doing.

A person on a wheelchair should not do this.

What will people say?

Clean it up.

Put it back again.

This time I put it to myself. Because I want to feel perfect from within. And that day I decided I am going to a life of myself. I am not going to be that perfect person for someone.

I am just going to take this moment and I will make it perfect for myself. And do you know, how we all begin?

That day I decided, I am going to fight my fears. We all have fears.

Fear of the unknown, fear of known.

Fear of losing people.

Fear of losing health, money.

We want to excel in a career.

We want to become famous.

We want to get money.

We are scared all the time.

so I wrote down one by one, all those fears. And I decided I am going to overcome those fears one at a time.

You know what was my biggest fear.

Divorce.

I couldn't stand this word.

I was trying to cling on this person who didn't want me anymore.

But I said no, I have to make it work.

But the day I decided that this is nothing but my fear.

I liberated myself by setting him free. And I made myself emotionally so strong that the day I got news that he is getting married, I sent him a text and said, 'I am so happy for you' and wanna wish you all the best. And he knows that I pray for him today.

My biggest fear number two was I won't be able to be a mother again and that was quite devastating for me.

But then I realize, there are so many children in the world, all they want is the acceptance. So there is no point of crying, just go and adopt one.

That's what I did.

I gave my name to different organizations, different orphanages. I didn't mention, I am on the wheelchair, dying to have a child. so I told then this is Muniba Mazari and she
wants to adopt, boy-girl what so ever. But I want to adopt and I waited patiently.

Two years later, I got this call from a very small city in Pakistan.

They said, 'Are you Muniba Mazari'?.

There is a baby boy.

Would you like to adopt?

And When I said 'Yes', I could literally feel the labor pain.

Yes Yes, I am going to adopt him. I am coming to take him home.

And when I reached there, the man was sitting there and he was looking at me from head to toe.

Don't judge me, I am in a wheelchair.

You know what he said, 'I know you will be the best mother of this child. You both will be lucky to have each other'. And that day, he was two days old and today he is six.

You will be surprised to know the bigger fear that I had in me.

It was facing people.

I used to hide from people. When I was in bed for two years and I used to keep the doors closed.

I used to pretend that I am not going to meet anyone. Tell them I am sleeping.

You know why?

Because I couldn't stand that sympathy that they had for me. They used to treat me like a patient.

When I used to smile, look at me and said, 'You are smiling, are you OK'.

I was tired of this question being asked.

Are you sick?

Well, a lady at the airport asked me, 'Are you sick'?.

And I said, well, besides this spinal cord injury, I am fine.

I guess.

Those were really cute questions.but, they never used to feel cute when I was on the bed. so I used to hide from people knowing that Oh my god I am not going to see that sympathy on their eyes.

It's all right.

Today, I am here speaking to all these amazing people.

Because I have overcome the fear.

You know when you ended up being in the wheelchair,
what's the most painful thing?

That's another fear.

People on the wheelchair, who are differently able to have their hearts but they never share. I will share that with you.

The lack of acceptance.

People think that they will not be accepted by the people because we and the world of perfect people are imperfects.

So, I decided instead of starting an INGO, NGO for disabilities awareness which I know will not help anyone, I started to appear more in public. I started to paint. I always wanted to. I have a lot of exhibitions for Pakistan, I have done a lot of modeling campaign, different campaign for brands like tony and guy.

I have done some really funny breaking the barriers kinds of modelings. There was this one by the name clown town where I became a clown because I know that clowns have a heart too.

So, when you accept yourself, the way you are, the world recognizes you. It all starts from within. I became the national goodwill ambassador of UN women, Pakistan. And now I speak for the rights of women and children.

We talk about inclusion, diversity, gender equality which is a must.

I was featured in BBC 100 women for 2015.

One of the Forbes 30 under 30 for 2016.

And it all didn't happen alone. You all are thriving in your careers. You have bigger dreams and aspirations in life. Always remember one thing, on the road to success there is always 'We' not 'Me'.

Do not think that you alone can achieve things.

No,

There is always another person, who is standing behind you, maybe not coming on the forefront, behind you, supporting you. Never lose that person.

Never.

No matter how much I say that I couldn't find a hero. so I became one. I still want to recognize those three people in my life who literally changed my life completely and I get inspiration from them every single day.

The women who believe in me even when I was completely on the verge of dis-pare where everybody left, she was there. And every time, I looked at her saying. She used to look at me and said, it's too shall pass. God has a bigger plan. One day you will say that Oh my God, that is why God has chosen me.

She never cried in front of me. She always said that there will be haters, there will be naysayers, there will be disbelievers and there will be you to proving them wrong.

My mother.

Whatever I am today, I am nothing without her. I am nothing without her. Thank you, mama, I wish you were here. Thank you for making me, who I am today.

You know, what we human being have a problem. We always expect each from lives.

We have this amazing fantasy about life.

This is how things should work.

This is my plan.

It should go as per my plan.

If that doesn't happen, we give up.

So my dear friends, let me tell you one thing. I never wanted to be in a wheelchair. Never thought of being in a wheelchair. I was always aspiring to do bigger things. and I had no idea, for that, I have to pay the price to be where I am today. It's a very heavy price.

This life is a test and a trial. Tests are trials. I never supposed to be easy and why you are expecting each from lives. And life gives you the lemon. and you made the lemonade. and then do not blame for life for that because you were expecting each from a trial.

Trial make you a stronger better person. Life is a trial. Every time you realize that.

It is OK to be scared.

It is OK to cry.

Everything is OK. but giving up is not be an option, should not be an option. They always say that failure is not an option. Failure should be an option. When you fail, you get up and then you fail, then you get up, that keeps you going. That's how humans are strong.

A failure is an option. It should be an option. but giving up is not.

Never.

We have these things in minds. We call it perfection. We want everything perfect. We want our self to be perfect. Perfect life, Perfect relationships, Perfect career, Perfect amount of money that we need to earn no matter what.

Nothing is perfect in this world. We all are perfectly imperfect. And that is perfectly alright. That's alright!

You were sent here not to become perfect people. Those people who tell you how to look perfect even those people are imperfect. Trying to fight this fear of looking imperfect. I used to be perfect. I still remember I got this complements, years ago, when I used to walk.

OMG, look at you, you are so fair, you are tall, you are perfect.

Look at me now.

Only the perfect eyes can see that.

Only the perfect eyes will see that.

Only the perfect eyes will see that.

So, Yes.

And all those imperfections you have to listen to your hearts.

You don't have to look good for people. You don't have to be perfect just because other people wanted you to be perfect. If your soul is perfect from within.

That's all right! This is all that you want. This is all that you need to be. Our society has made a very weird, very weird kind of norms to look perfect in grade.

For a man, it's different.

For a woman, it's different.

We think too much about what people say.

We listen to ourselves too little.

You know what makes you perfect.

When you make someone smile.

You know what makes you perfect when you try to do something good for the people around you.

You know what makes you perfect. when you feel someone's pain and how beautiful pain is that it connects with people. No other medium can connect you other but pain.

That's why I always say I am in pain.

That's a blessing for me.

Today, just because I am in pain and I am on the wheelchair, I work for children.

Being the head of CSRF of company we conduct medical camps in far-flung areas of Pakistan where so many kids died because there they don't have medical facilities.

And I personally believe that just because they cannot afford to live doesn't mean that we will let them die. so we give them money, we give them medical treatment. We try to heal their wounds. Physical and emotional.

And I also work for the beautiful people we call them third gender.

The transgender community of Pakistan.

You know, what connects me with them.

All my imperfections.

When I go and hug them they never judge me and this very good friend of mine. Her name is Bijli. Bijli means electricity.

And I said are you electricity.

She says 'no'.

I am lighting.

I am as strong as lightning.

I am thunder.

I am lightning.

She came to me and the first time I hugged she said You are just like me.

And I said I am like you.

Because to people, we are so imperfect. So how beautiful these imperfections are because of these imperfections, you can connect to people then why are we all running after being perfect.

What's the point?

Every time I go in public.

I smile.

And People asked me, 'Don't you get tired of smiling all the time' What's the secret.

I always say one thing.

I have stopped worrying about the things that I have lost, people I have lost. Things and people who were meant to be with me are with me and sometimes somebody's absence makes you a better person.

Cherish their absence.

It always a blessing.

I always say that people are so lucky that even they don't realize, you must be thinking.

OK.

You are lucky in that sense.

Well, the breath you just took now was a blessing.

Embraces it.

There are so many people in the world who are dreaming to live a life that you are living right now.

You have no idea.

Embraces each and every breath you are taking.

Celebrate your life.

Live it.

Don't die before your death.

We all die.

We live this one routine of the day for 75 years and we call it life.

No that's not life.

If you are still thinking about why you have been sent here.

If you are still juggling with the concept of why you are here, you haven't lived yet.

You work hard.

You make money.

You do it for yourself.

That's not life.

You go out and seek for people who need your help.

You make their lives better.

You add colors to their lives, you add values to their lives.

You become that sponge which removes all negativity.

You can become that person who can emit beautiful positive vibes and when you realize that you have changed someone's life and Because of you, this person didn't give up.

That is the day, when you live, Always.

We were talking about gratitude.

Why I smile all the time.

I cry all night when nobody sees me.

Because I am a human and I have to keep the balance. And I smiled all day because I know that if I smile I can make people smile, that keeps me going.

Be grateful, what you have. And you will always always always ended up with having more.

But if you will cry, if you will crip for the little things that you don't have or the things you have lost. You will never ever have enough. Sometimes we are too busy thinking about the things that we don't have.

Forget.

Cherish the blessings that we have. I am not saying that I am not healthy that makes me unlucky.

But Yes, it is hard. It is hard when I say I can't walk. It's hard when I say I have to wear that bag. It hurts. but I have to keep going. Because never giving up is the way to live. Always.

So well, end my talk, on a very short note.

Live your life fully. Accept the way you are. Be kind to yourself. Be kind to yourself.

I will repeat, Be kind to yourself. and then only we can be kind to others. Love your self. Spread that love. Life will be hard. There will be turmoil, there will be trials. But that will only make you stronger.

Never give up.

The real happiness does not lie in money of success or fame. I have all this and I have never wanted this.

Real happiness lies in gratitude. So be grateful and be alive and live in every moment.

Thank you so much, everyone

MALALA YOUSAFZAI

NOBLE PEACE PRIZE, OSLO, 2014

Bismillah hir rahman ir rahim.

In the name of God, the most merciful, the most beneficent. Your Majesties, Your royal highnesses, distinguished members of the Norweigan Nobel Committee.

Dear sisters and brothers, today is a day of great happiness for me. I am humbled that the Nobel Committee has selected me for this precious award. Thank you to everyone for your continued support and love. Thank you for the letters and cards that I still receive from all around the world. Your kind and encouraging words strengthen and inspire me.

I would like to thank my parents for their unconditional love. Thank you to my father for not clipping my wings and for letting me fly. Thank you to my mother for inspiring me to be patient and to always speak the truth - which we strongly believe is the true message of Islam. And also thank you to all my wonderful teachers,who inspired me to believe in myself and be brave.

I am proud, well, in fact, I am very proud to be the first Pashtun, the first Pakistani, and the youngest person to receive this award.

Along with that, along with that, I am pretty certain that I am also the first recipient of the Nobel Peace Prize who still fights with her younger brothers. I want there to be peace everywhere, but my brothers and I are still working on that.

I am also honored to receive this award together with Kailash Satyarthi, who has been a champion for children's rights for a long time. Twice as long, in fact, than I have been alive. I am proud that we can work together, we can work together and show the world that an Indian and a Pakistani, they can work together and achieve their goals of children's rights.

Dear brothers and sisters, I was named after the inspirational Malalai of Maiwand who is the Pashtun Joan of Arc. The word Malala means grief-stricken", sad", but in order to lend some happiness to it, my grandfather would always call me Malala
– The happiest girl in the world" and today I am very happy that we are together fighting for an important cause.

This award is not just for me. It is for those forgotten children who want an education. It is for those frightened children who want peace. It is for those voiceless children who want change. I am here to stand up for their rights, to raise their voice...

It is not time to pity them.

It is not time to pity them.

It is time to take action so it becomes the last time, the last time, so it becomes the last time that we see a child deprived of education.

I have found that people describe me in many different ways. Some people call me the girl who was shot by the Taliban. And some, the girl who fought for her rights. Some people, call me a "Nobel Laureate" now. However, my brothers still call me that annoying bossy sister.

As far as I know, I am just a committed and even stubborn person who wants to see every child getting a quality education, who wants to see women having equal rights and who wants peace in every corner of the world.

Education is one of the blessings of life—and one of its necessities. That has been my experience during the 17 years of my life. In my paradise home, Swat, I always loved learning and discovering new things. I remember when my friends and I would decorate our hands with henna on special occasions. And instead of drawing flowers and patterns we would paint our hands with mathematical formulas and equations.

We had a thirst for education, we had a thirst for education because our future was right there in that classroom. We would sit and learn and read together. We loved to wear neat and tidy school uniforms and we would sit there with big dreams in our eyes.

We wanted to make our parents proud and prove that we could also excel in our studies and achieve those goals, which some people think only boys can. But things did not remain the same. When I was in Swat, which was a place of tourism and beauty, suddenly changed into a place of terrorism.

I was just ten that more than 400 schools were destroyed. Women were flogged. People were killed. And our beautiful dreams turned into nightmares. Education went from being a right to being a crime. Girls were stopped from going to school. When my world suddenly changed, my priorities changed too.

I had two options.

One was to remain silent and wait to be killed. And the second was to speak up and then be killed.

I chose the second one.

I decided to speak up.

We could not just stand by and see those injustices of the terrorists denying our rights, ruthlessly killing people and misusing the name of Islam. We decided to raise our voice and tell them. Have you not learned, have you not learned that in the Holy Quran Allah says: if you kill one person it is as if you kill the whole humanity?

Do you not know that Mohammad, peace be upon him, the prophet of mercy, he says, do not harm yourself or others".

And do you not know that the very first word of the Holy Quran is the word Iqra", which means read"?

The terrorists tried to stop us and attacked me and my friends who are here today, on our school bus in 2012, but neither their ideas nor their bullets could win.

We survived.

And since that day, our voices have grown louder and louder.

I tell my story, not because it is unique, but because it is not. It is the story of many girls. Today, I tell their stories too.

I have brought with me some of my sisters from Pakistan, from Nigeria and from Syria, who share this story.

My brave sisters Shazia and Kainat who were also shot that day on our school bus. But they have not stopped learning. And my brave sister Kainat Soomro who went through severe abuse and extreme violence, even her brother was killed, but she did not succumb.

Also my sisters here, whom I have met during my Malala Fund

campaign. My 16-year-old courageous sister, Mezon from Syria, who now lives in Jordan as a refugee and goes from tent to tent encouraging girls and boys to learn.

And my sister Amina, from the North of Nigeria,where Boko Haram threatens, and stops girls and even kidnaps girls, just for wanting to go to school.

Though I appear as one girl, though I appear as one girl, one person, who is 5 foot 2 inches tall if you include my high heels. (It means I am 5 foot only) I am not a lone voice, I am not a lone voice, I am many.

I am Malala.

But I am also Shazia.

I am Kainat.

I am Kainat Soomro.

I am Mezon.

I am Amina.

I am those 66 million girls who are deprived of education. And today I am not raising my voice, it is the voice of those 66 million girls. Sometimes people like to ask me why should girls go to school, why is it important to them.

But I think the more important question is why shouldn't they, why shouldn't they have this right to go to school.

Dear sisters and brothers, today, in half of the world, we see rapid progress and development. However, there are many countries where millions still suffer from the very old problems of war, poverty, and injustice.

We still see conflicts in which innocent people lose their lives and children become orphans.

We see many people becoming refugees in Syria, Gaza, and Iraq. In Afghanistan, we see families being killed in suicide attacks and bomb blasts. Many children in Africa do not have access to education because of poverty. And as I said, we still see, we still see girls who have no freedom to go to school in the north of Nigeria. Many children in countries like Pakistan and India, as Kailash Satyarthi mentioned, many children, especially in India and Pakistan are

deprived of their right to education because of social taboos, or they have been forced
into child marriage or into child labor.

One of my very good school friends, the same age as me, who had always been a bold and confident girl, dreamed of becoming a doctor. But her dream remained a dream. At the age of 12, she was forced to get married. And then soon she had a son, she had a child when she herself was still a child – only 14. I know that she could have been a very good doctor. But she couldn't ... because she was a girl.

Her story is why I dedicate the Nobel Peace Prize money to the Malala Fund, to help give girls quality education, everywhere, anywhere in the world and to raise their voices.

The first place this funding will go to is where my heart is, to build schools in Pakistan—especially in my home of Swat and Shangla. In my own village, there is still no secondary school for girls. And it is my wish and my commitment, and now my challenge to build one so that my friends and my sisters can go there to school and get a quality education and to get this opportunity to fulfill their dreams.

This is where I will begin, but it is not where I will stop. I will continue this fight until I see every child, every child in school.

Dear brothers and sisters, great people, who brought change, like

Martin Luther King and Nelson Mandela, Mother Teresa and Aung San Suu Kyi, once stood here on this stage.

I hope the steps that Kailash Satyarthi and I have taken so far and will take on this journey will also bring change – lasting change. My great hope is that this will be the last time, this will be the last time we must fight for education.

Let's solve this once and for all.

We have already taken many steps. Now it is time to take a leap. It is not time to tell the world leaders to realize how important education is - they already know it - their own children are in good schools. Now it is time to call them to take action for the rest of the world's children. We ask the world leaders to unite and make education their top priority.

Fifteen years ago, the world leaders decided on a set of global goals, the Millennium Development Goals. In the years that have followed, we have seen some progress. The number of children out of school has been halved, as Kailash Satyarthi said. However, the world focused only on primary education, and progress did not reach everyone. In the year 2015, representatives from all around the world will meet in the United Nations to set the next set of goals, the Sustainable Development Goals.

This will set the world's ambition for the next generations. The world can no longer accept, the world can no longer accept that basic education is enough.

Why do leaders accept that for children in developing countries, only basic literacy is sufficient, when their own children do homework in Algebra, Mathematics, Science, and Physics?

Leaders must seize this opportunity to guarantee a free, quality, primary and secondary education for every child. Some will say this is impractical, or too expensive, or too hard. Or maybe even impossible. But it is time the world thinks bigger.

Dear sisters and brothers, the so-called world of adults may understand it, but we children don't.

Why is it that countries which we call strong" are so powerful in creating wars but are so weak in bringing peace?

Why is it that giving guns is so easy but giving books is so hard?

Why is it, why is it that making tanks is so easy, but building schools are so hard?

We are living in the modern age and we believe that nothing is impossible.

We have reached the moon 45 years ago and maybe will soon land on Mars.

Then, in this 21st century, we must be able to give every child quality education.

Dear sisters and brothers, dear fellow children, we must work... not wait. Not just the politicians and the world leaders, we all need to contribute.

Me.

You.

We.

It is our duty.

Let us become the first generation to decide to be the last, let us become the first generation that decides to be the last that sees empty classrooms, lost childhoods, and wasted potentials.

Let this be the last time that a girl or a boy spend their childhood in a factory.

Let this be the last time that a girl is forced into early child marriage.

Let this be the last time that a child loses life in war.

Let this be the last time that we see a child out of school.

Let this end with us.

Let's begin this ending ... together ... today ... right here, right now.

Let's begin this ending now.

Thank you so much.

NICK VUICIC

Speech on How to stop a Bully.

How you guys doing? Good, good good good good.

Well guys, I was born this way, and there's no medical reason why that happened. My brother and my sister were born with arms and legs.

And sometimes in life, things happen that don't make sense. My doctors never thought that I'd be able to walk, and today, I'm walking. I'm from Australia, anybody want to one day go to Australia? It's such a cool place. And I now live in LA; I'm a Southern California boy. So I only live about four hours from here.

And today I'm going to tell you, man — I love freaking people out. One day I'm in a car, I'm in the front seat — I'm not driving of course. Can you imagine if I'm driving a car? They reckon they can put a joystick — that

thing that controls my wheelchair —
we can put that in a car.

Like how fully sick is that?

Imagine if I get pulled over by the
cops? Can I have your driver's license
please? Yeah, but, it's over there;
you're going to have to get it.

Imagine if I'm in big trouble! Put your
hands up! Uhhhh.. Get out of your
car! Uhhhhh...

So I'm in the front passenger's seat,
we're at the traffic lights, and this car
comes up next to us and this girl's
looking at me. And I'm looking at her,
she's looking at me, I'm looking at her,
she's looking at me, I'm looking at her.
All she sees is my head, right? She
has no idea that I have no arms and
no legs. So I'm thinking, cool.

I'm going to freak you out.

So I get the seatbelt in my mouth, and I loosen it like this, so that I can freely move. And she's looking at me like "why are you eating your seatbelt?' So I pull it, the belt is loose, I can move.

Now she's looking at me, full 100% attention and focus. And just imagine all you see is my head, all right? You might want to put up your hand to your face to cut off the rest of my body. So you can really see the effect, so...That's it, exactly.

Here we go, ready? I just did this. And her face, man. She was like — she nearly ran the red light, man. It was so good.

My parents always said, Nick, you don't know what you can achieve until you try it. And the doctors looked at me and said, he's not going to walk, he's not going to go to school, he's not going to do anything in his life.

And then my parents; they just loved me like crazy, and said you've got to try. Try this, try that, try this, try that, and I'm thinking sometimes, like, Mom and Dad, you're crazy, I have no arms and no legs. How would I ever be able to do this or do that?

But they encouraged me, and they loved me. And as human beings, we're waiting for stuff like that, we all want love. Everybody say it — looooove. Very good.

We all want love. I went to school, and I wanted to be cool, you know. You go to school and you want to be accepted. So, you see these guys, and you're like, oh man, you know?

Everyone swears, like every third sentence. F this, and F that, and F'n this, and F F, like, what, they think they're cool,
you know. And so I'm thinking, maybe I need to be like them to be cool.

And then you compare each other with how we look and I wish I was smarter, I wish I was taller, I wish I was shorter, I wish I was more popular, I wish I did this, I wish I didn't have that. I wish my life was different.That was me when I was about 8 years old; I looked at myself, and I looked at everybod else, and everyone else had more than me. And I'm asking, why? Why me? Have you ever asked the why me questions, but get nowhere?

If I had no answers from the doctors, and if I had no answers from my parents, I still have a choice, every day in my life, to keep going or give up. You see this book up here?

This is my favorite book in the whole wide world. This is my favorite book, the bible. And here I am – and here I am, and for me, that's my full potential in all that I can be here on earth. And so encouragement takes me closer to all that I can be, and discouragement takes me away.

You see, it only takes three seconds for someone to tease me when I was at school, and just say ewwwww, you're ugly. Ewww, you can't do this and you can't do that. Some of you are thinking, like, man, seriously? You had kids picking on you? How heartless are those kids? Picking on me with no limbs? You would probably say, well, I'm not that bad. I wouldn't pick on a kid with no limbs. But why would you pick on anyone? Well, because it's fun, it's just culture. OK, we'll

get to that.

But for me, facing all that stuff? I'm getting these seeds, everyone say seeds, S-E-E-D-S, seeds. Have you seen the pictures of the sequoia reds up here in California? These huge trees. Like some of the trunks could be nearly as big as this room. I've seen those photos where they've actually dug out a tunnel in a trunk of a tree — you can drive a full-size SUV right through it. That all started with a little seed.

If you leave a seed of lies in your heart and in your mind, and you don't know the truth? If you don't know the truth, you will die with the lie. I started dying, because I started believing what I was told.

I want you to know the three things that I needed to come to in my life is the truth of my values, the truth of my purpose, and the truth of my destiny. I want you to know something. In our mind, we put ourselves down all the time. I want to ask you today, do you think I'm cool enough to be your friend? But I don't swear, I don't use the F-bomb, am I still cool enough to be your friend? But I don't tease people, am I still cool enough to be your friend? But I have no arms and no legs. Seriously.

You would be my friend, even though I have no arms, no legs. So you're telling me it actually doesn't matter, right? If it actually doesn't matter, for how we look, then why do we tease one another for how we look if it actually doesn't matter? Why is it that?

We look ourselves in the mirror, and we say, well, we're having fun! Oh yeah, man it's just part of culture, man.

There were twelve people one day teased me.Taking me away from my hope. 12, 11, 10, 9, 8, 7, 6, 5, 4, 3, 2, 1. Don't worry, I won't fall off, because if I did, I'd break my arm.

But twelve people teased me one day. And I can put a pretty brave face on but cry on the inside. For real. Oh, it doesn't hurt!

Yeah, it hurts. There was this one bully,

I became his target for three weeks. And every time I'd go by him — I was 13, he was 17. I was in my chair. I'm only 4'9" in my other chair, my old chair. He's like 6' something, so he's huge, right? So I'm looking up at him, and every time I'd go by him, he's like, "Hey, there's Nick! He has no..." And you can imagine what he said. And I'm like, what's his problem, man?

So I would try to avoid him, and I was so embarrassed, because he would say it really loud and everybody would be looking and some would be laughing. I'm like, what is this guy's problem, man? So one day, after three weeks, I went up to him and I said, "Hey".

He's like, "Hey".

And I said, "Can you please stop it?"

He said, "Stop what?"

I said "Stop teasing me".

He said, "What are you talking about?"

I said, "Every time I walk by you say that stuff".

He's like, "What stuff?" He didn't know how to take me on.

So I'm looking up at him and said, "No man. Every time I walk by, you say exactly this, and I want you to stop. I forgive you, but stop it".

He's like, "Oh, it's not hurting you".

Now, I could have said, "No," or I could have said yeah. It takes a level of humility to actually say, um, actually, I don't like that. It's killing me.

And I said, "Ah,

yeah, it's hurting me".

He said, "All right, I'm sorry man. I was just, you know, playing around".

I said, "Give me a hug".

He said, "What?"

I said, "Give me a hug".

He's like, "All right". So I gave him a hug. I'm a hugging machine. We made the Guinness Book of World Records: 1,749 hugs in one year. We did it last year — my arms fell off, all right?

The scary thing about hugging so many people is that anyone can just pick me up and take me home. Like, what am I going to do, like, –hit them or something?

Pretty mean head-butt, right?

I want you to know that you might be playing around. I can pretty much say that 98% of you have teased someone in your life. I tried to commit suicide because of people who thought they were having fun, not knowing the hell that I was going through.

The people you're teasing — what if the person you're teasing
is the person who's thinking of committing suicide.

What if the person you're teasing is the one who's trying to commit suicide, who hates their life because of you? You don't know if the person you are teasing is the son or daughter of a drunk at home getting abused. And all they need is someone like you to keep on pushing them this way.

We need hope, so find something else to do. Find positive things in your own life; I don't care about how you look, I will never ever ever tease you. I

will never tease you! I could tease you,
I could be tough.

People thinking that bullying is tough?
It ain't tough! My wheelchair? This is
tough. This thing, man, I'll tell you
something — you ready?

This wheelchair. This thing's so tough.
When my friend built this for me, he
said, you're going to love it. I said
what, does
it go fast? He said no, but it's tough.
And I said, well, what do you mean?
He said, you'll find out.

The torque in these motors, at the
bottom at the back. This thing. If
someone's holding it. I'm telling you,
it can go 90 degrees. I went 80
degrees up, alright? Someone's

holding me to make sure I don't tip back.

My wife, she loves shopping with me, because she just jumps on the back, and we go shopping. She just shops and shops, because she doesn't drop, right? We just go and do it; it's fun.

Now what I tried one day to do — you'll never believe me, maybe you will, just know that every word that comes out of my mouth is not an exaggeration.

One day, I needed to move a car. So I got my wife to put my car, my '66 Chevelle, in neutral. It's a two and a half ton car,
and I backed it back with this thing. Two and a half — just this. Just like this, like nothing. This thing is tough.

Guess what?

The definition of tough means it's strong. To show your strength, you need to do something that's difficult. I would sound so stupid if I said hey guys, I got a matchbox car one day, and I got some fishing line, and I towed that matchbox car all around all day.

How tough is my BMW? That's stupid.

That's the same thing with bullying. You think you're tough?

You're trying to show your strength? That's not your strength.

Let me come back in ten years and let me get your three — anyone have a three year old nephew? Anyone have a three year old nephew?

Cool. Put your hands down.

I will get any one of your three year old nephews, bring them tomorrow night at where I'm speaking, and we're going to put them up on stage, and let me show you how tough I am. We'll get your three year old nephew, and we'll put him up here, on the table, and let me tease him. Let me show you how
tough I am.

That's what you are! I could pick on you, you biggest bullies. I could pick on anything you like. Any singer, any music that you like. I could tease you, I could tease your family, I could tease your friends, I could tease about the movies you think are really cool, I could tease anything about you.

I could tease you about your nose, your eyes, your teeth, your chin, your hair, your ears, your elbows, your knees, your whatever, man! I can tease you about anything. It ain't hard, just like you can tease me.

You want to know what tough is? Go to the people you tease, and say sorry. You want to know what tough is, go up to the people who still tease you, and say, hey. Stop it, I forgive you, but please stop it. That's tough.

I want you to know something, the truth of who you are. I don't care what job you get.

I don't care. I don't care how smart you are, everyone. I don't care. I don't care,

I love you and I believe in you. I don't care if you end up being a janitor in this school, I'll tell you why – because the janitor in my high school inspired me to be a speaker. He changed my life. He said, you should be a speaker, you know, and I said, you're crazy! He said no really, you need to be a speaker.

I said, stop it man. Four months later, he twisted my arm, and I said yes. I spoke in front of ten people, then another ten, then another ten, then I found myself in front of 300 sophomore students. And three minutes into my speech, half the girls were crying, and one girl in the middle of the room started weeping. She put up her hand and said "I'm so sorry, can I come up there and give you a hug." And in front of everybody, she came up and she hugged me, and she cried on my shoulder, and she whispered in this ear. Thank you, thank you, thank you, no one's ever told me that they love me. No one's ever told me that I'm beautiful the way that I am.

It was because my parents told me that I was beautiful that I am still here. Some of you don't have those parents, and that's why I'm here. I love you and you're beautiful just the way you are. Never, ever give up.

How many schools do you think that I spoke to actually stopped bullying altogether? OK.

Whoever said one, you are correct. One school out of 600, I got a letter from the headmaster, and he said Nick, you forever changed our school, blah blah blah. We haven't seen any bullies pick on anybody for eight months straight. We don't know what happened, but in the best words that I can describe, there's just a new thought in the air that it just ain't cool anymore. It just ain't cool.

I want to ask you: What are you going to do? Are you going to continue on? At the risk of knowing that in each section, this section, right here, five people already tried to commit suicide. That section there? Five people. When you extrapolate it out? What if the person you're teasing is one of those and you have

no idea. Would you find something else to do?

So, the change is up to you. If you want to see more love in your school, be love. If 50% of the school come together and say you know what, it just ain't cool anymore the people who think it's still cool, every time they look down upon you, I want you to look up. I want you to imagine my face looking at you. Because I'm telling you, everyone you're teasing is my brother and my sister. And you're my brother, and you're my sister.

And I'm asking you to stop.

Love yourself a bit more, love each other a lot more.

DWAYNE JOHNSON 'THE ROCK' : Be Yourself

The Rock: Thank you, Oprah, for having me.

Thank you, guys.

Oprah: So, your father was very strict. Now, here's the thing.

You've gone one on one with some fierce competitors in the ring, right? But now you were in one of the scariest situations
any man can be in raising three daughters.

The Rock: Yes. Yes, extremely scary.

Oprah: And are you a strict Dad?

The Rock: I am. Not super strict, but discipline is important. But also, you know, I'll go back to my dad. My dad loved me with a small capacity in which he was capable of. So, I learned from that and so with my daughters, I want to be as full and as present with the love that I give them.

Oprah: Present, yes. That's what we were talking about. What do you want to make sure that they get that you didn't get? And it's so interesting when you have children, I've seen this from a lot of people who, you didn't get what you needed.

You just didn't get what you needed because of what The Rock just said, your parents didn't have the capacity to give it to you.

And now that you're older, you have to learn to give that to yourself and to be able to give that to your children in a way that you don't carry on what was done to you.

So, what is it you want your daughters to know about the way you love them?

The Rock: I want my daughters to know that I love them unconditionally, truly, unconditionally without condition. And I have a daughter who's 18 years old, her name is Simone.

Jasmine who just turned four, baby, Tiana, thank you who is getting ready to turn two.

And I am as I told my 18-year-old daughter, Simone, I said I love you. I'm going to tell you I love you every day, I'm going to text you I love you...

Oprah: So, you're one of those who say the words out loud?

The Rock: Yes, because I didn't get that. And I look at you, I love you and I'm going to text you. But I also told her, I'm unattached. You don't even have to text me back. Right?

You could text me back.

It's fine. But you don't have to, like it's okay. It's without condition. It's unconditional love.

And I also want to teach my daughters the value of hard work. More importantly, I want to teach my daughters the value of being kind, and how important that is.

Oprah: Well, you know, I read that your father, you used to watch him in training, and he would say, "If I'm going to get up at 6:00 AM, you're going to get up at 6:00 AM."

So, what do you think you've got the most from him?

Was it your work ethic?

What was it?

The Rock: It was definitely my work ethic. My dad was a man who, against the odds, made it. But he would get up at usually 5:00, 5:30 in the morning, and he would say if I get up, you're going to get up too. He would drag me to the gym and by the way, I'm five years old, and he would drag me to the gym.

Yes.

And I wouldn't work out, but he would just make sure that I was there and be with him, and that was our time that we could spend together. But I would say my work ethic from my dad, my dad always said too that, regardless of what you do in life and where you go, respect is going to be given when it's earned.

And you have to go out and earn it every single day.

Oprah: Yeah.

So, your dad taught you a lot. I wonder, what have your daughters taught you?

The Rock: My daughters taught me how to be I think more caring and more sensitive and more selfless.

Oprah: Yeah. Were you there for all of them when they were born?

The Rock: I was right there.

Oprah: Right there?

The Rock: I mean, right there.

Yes.

Oprah: I mean, you were right there.

The Rock: I was right there.

Yes.

And bring it on.

I mean, this is our moment.

Yes.

Oprah: Yeah.

Yeah.

And is that a life-changing moment, when that happens for you?

The Rock: It's the greatest thing that I have ever experienced in my life.

And it gave me such a profound respect for my babies' mamas.

I have two.

I was once married and now I'm happily married.

Lauren is back there.

We've known each other for 13 years now but I have, it has been the most profound experience of my life because also too, you know, when you meet...

As a man, you meet someone, you meet a woman, and this is going to be the one and you want to get married and my first marriage didn't work out.

But then the birth of a child and what that does and the lens perspective that just shifts and it just gives me a new profound respect for again, their moms as...

Oprah: So, it didn't work out with the marriage, but then she became your business partner, your first marriage?

The Rock: She did.

Yes, yes.

Oprah: And you still are.

The Rock: We still are.

So, my ex-wife, Dany, we, the marriage didn't work out.

And it was just one of those things where it wasn't an ugly divorce, it was just marriage wasn't in our cards. We're great friends. Marriage wasn't in our cards, but we both had an appetite for business and to accomplish things.

And we thought, "Well, what if we continued to do business together and do you think we can?"

And it felt like we could make something happen and we did.

Oprah: I know you didn't grow up with a lot of money. And I read the story about when, I think you were 15, and there was an eviction notice on the door and how that made a big impression on you, right?

The Rock: It did.

Yes.

Oprah: Now, you're one of the highest-paid actors in the world.

The Rock: Thank you.

I do all right. Thank you.

Oprah: You do all right.

And does that title, the sexiest man alive, the highest paid in the... What do those titles mean if anything?

You're the greatest, you're the most popular, you're the most followed, you're the most, you're the most, the most, the most, the most.

The Rock: It's great for the ego. It's wonderful.

Oprah: Yeah, the better question is, how do you keep your ego in check when all of that is happening around?

The Rock: Sure. Very important. People I have around me and how important that is...

Oprah: Do you have anybody who can tell you the truth at this point?

The Rock: Yeah, she's called my wife. Yes.

Oprah: Okay. Lauren can tell you the truth?

The Rock: Yes, Lauren can tell me the truth. But by the way, and this is where it's the tricky thing for us to being in this position, is we want to make sure that we have people around us who are inspired to do well and reach for and continue to share our vision, but also at time say, well, I'm not quite sure if that's the right thing to do.

So, look, I've had a wonderful career, especially coming from being evicted. And those titles are nice, and everything is fine. But honestly, I'm so grateful to be in the position I'm in and I never take anything for granted.

I try not to...

Oprah: Aren't you glad that you were once evicted, because it gives you such an appreciation for what you have now?

The Rock: It just gives such perspective. When we were 14 years old, we lived in Hawaii and we lived in a small efficiency apartment.

And we were, my mom and I came home, and I'll never forget the rent was $180 a week.

And there was an eviction...

Oprah: A week?

The Rock: A week.

And that was an eviction notice on the door. And it was, this was the one, it was the final eviction notice, like, that's the one. My mom started crying, and I never forgot in that moment, it was a seminal moment for me because I felt like I never want to be in this position again.

What can I do?

So, at 14 years old, I thought, well, the heroes in my life, Muhammad Ali, for example, professional wrestlers, they're all men who have worked hard with their hands and they built their body.

Yes, that's what I'm gonna do. I'm gonna do what my dad taught me and these other heroes, I'm gonna go build my body so, we're never evicted again, but being evicted, by the way, has as you were saying has not only given me just great perspective, but also great gratitude, but also my team and my family, we laugh at it, but I feel this way like, "Oh, well, you know, we're a month away from being evicted. I gotta go to work." Like, I still have that in my head.

Oprah: You still have that?

The Rock: I still have that in my head, you know, but it keeps you grounded by the way. Yeah, because that's why the most this and the most that again, it's wonderful. But the alternative is what I once was.

Oprah: And it also doesn't change the way you're wired because I still save toast.

I do.

I will save a toast rather than throw it away. And I know there's going to be more toast, but I still do because there's something in me because when we were growing up, we had to save it.

You know, you weren't allowed to like throw food away.

So, that was a really big deal.

So, here's the deal.

You have now the... you get the biggest paychecks, you have all this money, acclaim, fame, you didn't have that growing up.

How do you raise children who have good sense, and are also kind when they have everything?

Because part of what made you who you are, is having had that eviction notice and having not had everything.

So, how do you do that, how are you planning to do that with your children?

The Rock: So, for example, with our 18-year-old daughter, it was really important that we share those stories, share the stories about being evicted.

Her mom's parents were immigrants who came over from Cuba.

It's important that we've always shared those stories and also, we live, we try and keep it as simple as we possibly can.

I live, we have a farm in Virginia, happily to say that I've moved my family here to Atlanta,

so...

Oprah: Yaay!

The Rock: Place 30, 45 minutes away where it's very quiet, but also just making sure that we continue to instill in the babies and the kids the value of $1 and what it means and the value of food and always saying how grateful we are and the things that we're grateful for, especially at that young age.

Oprah: So, I want to know, how is success different from the way you imagined it would be?

The Rock: I never imagined this. I, at one time when I was a kid, I did feel in my heart and in my gut, that I was... that I thought, I think the world's going to hear from me.

I don't know how, but I do feel that way.

But I never thought in my mind, it was this level of success or fame even. It was, I don't know how but the world is going to hear from me.

So, you know, which is maybe why you know, at times, I could walk around and I could look at things like I'm a big kid, like everything can at times can be like I'm in Willy Wonka's

Chocolate Factory, where I'm just really in awe of everything that's really happening around me.

Oprah: What's the first thing you splurged on when you realize you had enough to splurge?

The Rock: Okay.

So, all right.

The first thing I splurged on, so when I was a kid, 14 years old, 13, 14 years old, in my mind, what it meant to be successful, it was a Rolex watch, right.

So, there was such a valuable lesson out of this. So, I thought for years oh, wait, everyone, every successful man has a Rolex watch and has diamonds in it.

So, when I finally was making a little bit of money, and this was in 1999, and I thought, okay, and by the way, I was still living in an apartment paying monthly rent but again.

Oprah: Oh, you renting and buying a Rolex?

The Rock: I was just renting, horrible financial...

Oprah: You should definitely if you're buying
a Rolex, okay.

The Rock: Yes. This is what not to do. So, I thought, this is it.

I'm gonna splurge and I went, and I got myself a Rolex.

And I wore it at that time I was wrestling. I was in the ring, not for a match, but I was doing an interview in the ring.

And I wore it in the ring and a melee broke out, which always happens in the wild world of professional wrestling.

One of the wrestlers fell on the Rolex when it came off, it broke, live TV and you see me, "Oh my gosh, my Rolex."

And I'm supposed to be in the moment and wrestling these other guys.

"Oh, no.

My Rolex."

Like, you can see the tape I'm trying to get my Rolex and somebody's like kicking me in the ribs while I'm trying to get it.

So, I finally got my Rolex back.

I go backstage, I look at it, I'm heartbroken now.

This is my thing.

And I go home that night and I remember immediately thinking this is a sign.

And I...

Oprah: Oh, I believe in signs, you know.

The Rock: Yes, it's a sign and I don't need it. And it wasn't right for me at that time, and I never got anything like that again.

Oprah: And so now do you just, do splurge carefully?

The Rock: I do.

I'm not a big bling guy or anything like that. And I always want to just make sure that now the splurge is usually with property.

Like we have two properties that way, because...

Oprah: I believe in real estate.

The Rock: Yes, Yes, you do.

Yes.

Oprah: I do, I Yes.

I love property the way some women love shoes, you know?

I do.

I do.

Because God isn't making any more land.

Okay.

The Rock: That's right.

Oprah: This is what we got here on the planet Earth. You're not getting any more.

The Rock: Yeah, that's right.

And also, the properties are our anchor. It's where we could be comfortable. And so that and I have a few pickup trucks. That's it.

Oprah: Just a few.

So, I remember reading this, that it was like Wrestle Mania 13 and you're still being called Rocky.

And there were a bunch of fans at the time who were jeering you and they were saying unkind things. And you used that moment and literally turned on your heels and turned it around. And you know, this whole vision tour is about people who've been knocked down sometimes in life, everybody, you know, not in a ring, but have had those moments where you didn't feel like the rest of the world saw you for who you needed to be.

How were you able to turn that around?

The Rock: Okay.

So, thank you for bringing that up. So, this is, it was a turning point in my career, and it really allowed me to grow. And it really allowed me just to be me and be anchored in with who I am.

So, when I first started wrestling, the idea was, well, why don't you call yourself Rocky

Maivia out of respect for your dad, Rocky Johnson, and your grandfather, Peter Maivia.

I hated the name.

And I thought well, I just wanted to make my own way.

And I wanted to be independent.

I love my family, but I don't want to do it like that because it feels like I'm trying to leverage their fame.

The powers that be said, "No, that's your name."

I was also told, well, when you go out and you wrestle, you have to smile.

I want you to smile big.

This is in the WWE.

Oprah: Why are you smiling if you...

The Rock: Because the idea was, I was a rookie in the wrestling business.

I was a, what's called the wrestling business as a term called baby face, which is a good guy.

I was being groomed as a good guy, wrestler, young.

The idea was you're grateful, grateful for the opportunity so when you go out there, I want you to smile. You can't smile enough.

And I thought, "Well, what if I lose?

Nope.

Yes, exactly.

You still gotta smile and it just didn't feel right.

That didn't sit right with me.

So, a few months later, the company made me the Intercontinental Champion. And then a month later we go into the annual biggest event.

It's like the Super Bowl of wrestling, Wrestle Mania and it was Wrestle Mania 13. By the time I got to Chicago Wrestle Mania,
16,000 people in the middle of the ring when I was in the ring and I'm supposed to be a good guy and they're supposed to cheer me;

16,000 people were chanting, "Rocky sucks".

Thank you for laughing, the few of you.

But it was...

Oprah: Can you hear the word sucks clearly when you're on the mat Rocky sucks?

The Rock: Yes.

Oprah: Yeah, Rocky sucks.

The Rock: There's a reverb that happens in the arena.

And when in unison, not one person, "You suck."

16,000.

And I was, I remember laying there in the ring and the referee said to me, "Don't look to them" And it was crippling for me.

So, then, at that time, the powers that be thought, this isn't going to work. And for whatever reason, people are not liking you, and they're not connecting with you.

And so, in that moment, it was very defining because I asked them if I could just be myself and if I could go out there, and if I can speak to the crowd, and if I could just be myself and be authentic.

And if I don't want to smile, I don't smile.

If I want to laugh, I laugh.

If I want to sing, I sing whatever it is, I just want to be me.

Can I have that for one minute of live TV time?

The powers that be at that time, Vince McMahon said, "You got it."

So, on Raw live TV, I grabbed a microphone and I said, "I may be a lot of things but sucks isn't one of them."

And I said something to the effect of basically it's not a this thing, it's not a that thing, it's a me being myself thing.

And before you know it, I guess the moral of the story is the importance and the power of finding your identity and being true to who you are.

Even in that wild world of pro wrestling, it still applies to everyone in the room, and how powerful that could be because there was a true shift and click moment.

And I never looked back and I became, fortunately, the biggest draw that the business has ever seen.

Oprah: Wow. You know, I was talking earlier about intention,
and you have acquired and continue to acquire a lot as you're continuing to build Seven Bucks.

What is the purest, highest, truest intention behind it all?

Because I know, at the end of the day, it isn't all about fame and it isn't all about making money. So, the reason why you want to continue to grow and succeed is what?

The Rock: To create an amazing experience for people. And that's important to me because that's an opportunity that I have to give joy and help, whether it transforms or a movie or a thing or whatever it is like the audience's experience, audience experience is something that's deeply personal to me.

And I think that goes back to when I would, so before the bright lights of the WWE, I was wrestling in a small wrestling company.

I would wrestle in flea markets and use car dealerships. You put a ring in the used car dealership in the parking lot, but the reason why I bring that up and state fairs, but there was an intimacy there and even at that level, it was always about well, how can I send the audience home happy and make people feel good?

And by the way, I also feel like if you're in a position to make people feel good, that is such a powerful thing. It's such a powerful.

Oprah: Yeah. I know we did you for a masterclass for OWN and something you said really stuck with me, that the most powerful thing you can ever do is to be yourself.

The Rock: Be yourself. Yes.

Oprah: And you were talking about that earlier, about that moment that you learned to be authentic is when everything changed.

The Rock: That's when everything changed. It's like a shift and click moment when we, for me when I realize there's great power and being myself, same thing for all of us.

But I do.

I believe it's the most powerful thing that we could be. It's easier said than done because I struggled for a long time trying to figure out well,

what's my identity?

And who am I?

And, for example, when I got to Hollywood, the very first time I got to Hollywood in the early 2000s, I was told, again, well,
if you want to be a star, then maybe you shouldn't talk about wrestling, maybe you shouldn't go to the gym as much, maybe you shouldn't raise your silly eyebrow.

And you know, there was a lot of things like that, and when you don't know you buy into it.

And so, I thought, okay, well maybe...

So, don't call yourself The Rock.

Okay.

So, again, I went through that in process for years trying to figure out who I was. And then when you look back at my earlier career, the films I was doing, they were good, but just not, you know, like "Oh, that's how I like to see him because he is his true authentic self."

Oprah: And have you had a sweet revenge moment?

The Rock: Yeah, who sucks now, huh?

Yeah.

Oprah: One of those.

The Rock: One of those.

Yes, it was...

Okay.

So, at this time when I felt like okay, I really need to make a change in my career, I need to be me, and I want to have the kind of career that is a global career.

And I said, I am not quite sure how we're going to do it. But I need you to buy into the vision with me and I'm willing to put in the work with my own two hands as I was telling my agency at that time in Hollywood.

And they all looked at me like I had three heads and they thought, well, we just don't... They've thought, okay, sure, sure, sure, sure, kind of placating me.

And then eventually I'd left them and then decided, you know what?

My name is The Rock and I come from the world of professional wrestling. And I look the way I look. And I talk the way I talk, and I love to work out.

And you know what, this is who I'm going to be.

And then here I am today.

So, for those who said, we don't get it, kind of sweet revenge.

Oprah: So, you posted on Instagram in November, "Joy and hope cost nothing" remember this?

The Rock: Yes.

Oprah: And yet, it's the most powerful gift that we can all give. And that's the real magic to life.

So, after everything that you've been through, particularly this past week, what are you now most grateful for today?

The Rock: I'm most grateful for life. I'm most grateful for an opportunity, I'm most grateful for my family. I'm most... Gratitude is a big thing with me. I mean, it is truly my anchor.

Yes...

Oprah: Mine too.

The Rock: It's my anchor, and I wake up with a heart full of gratitude, and even in death and even when things don't go right and even though I didn't make it to the NFL me, making it to the NFL was the best thing that never happened.

Yes. Because it also gave me a great sense of gratitude to be here. So, I would say that it would be... And also, I want to tell you, and I'll tell you this Oprah, and I want to tell you guys like I was so excited to come here and do this with you and share a little bit of my story and background and any kind of wisdom that I have learned over the years to share with you guys.

But I want you to know that especially this week of just, you know, laying my dad to rest I needed this from you, and I thank you, truly.

Thank you.

Oprah: Thank you.

Thank you.

The Rock: Thank you.

Thank you so much.

I did.

I love you back, I truly do.

Oprah: That's a good mana y'all just gave. It's a good mana.

The Rock: Thank you. I did. I needed this and I needed this.

I needed the love and this mana because what I also realized is and I felt it coming in is that you know you go to Rock concerts and things and events and wrestling matches or whatever.

But you know, when you come to this room and you have thousands, 12, 13, 15,000 people who have one intention which is to be better and give so much love and receive so much love, it's a powerful thing.

Oprah: Yeah, it is a very powerful thing. Thank you for being here today to share it.

R. <u>MADHAVAN</u>

<u>India in 2030</u>

So, first of all, thank you very much for having me here at the Inspire Series. It's worked dramatically, I'm already inspired to be addressing this really August intellectual gathering of people from Harvard, a place that my mother thought I will never reach.

But you know what, lot of people have spoken before me and eloquently and described their dreams for India and given figures and facts that either are skeptical and like, Mr. Omar says, aspirational.

But I'm just an actor and I'm going to just give you my dream shamelessly, because that's the thing that I can do best.

And by that, I mean when we talk of dreams we have one of our greatest scientists and philanthropists Dr. Abdul Kalam, and he said something which is very interesting.

He said, "Dreams are not what you have when you sleep.

The true dreams are the ones that don't let you sleep".

He said, "When you have that dream once it's a dream; when you have it twice it becomes a desire.

And when you see it for the third time consecutively, it becomes a passion, an aim and a goal", and that is the passion with which I want to see this fantasy that I have for India 2030.

And Abraham Lincoln also was a dreamer and you know, but he said one thing that makes most sense in trying to achieve this goal that I have dreamed for my nation.

He said, "If I have six hours to cut down a tree, then I would spend the first four hours sharpening the axe."

There's a great philosophy in that.

In this era of instant gratification we just keep thinking we can achieve all these goals by just tweaking this, tweaking that, it's not true.

I really believe that a missionary zeal is required to make that quantum change, that can make 2030 of what I'm dreaming about right now.

And just let's look at India as a country, what a unique nation!

Seriously.

Thousands of years old of culture and tradition, many many invasions, being ruled for many years and we still somehow managed to maintain our identity.

We still somehow have managed to maintain our Indian-ness — our beliefs, our faith and you know, yeah, there has been — we have our drawbacks — there is corruption, there is violence, there is differences between the different religions and sects and caste and everything.

But I can't help but think looking at India at the geography that we're not doing really that bad.

Look at all the other nations around in the world.

Look at our neighbors, compared to that there is somebody in India who's doing something right for us to be called a growing economy and being projected as the third largest economy in 2026 and the most educated and young nation in the world, it's still functional democracy.

So let's first accept the fact that there is somebody, some people in India with the right ideas and the ability to lead the nation to where we are today.

Under that assumption — under that assumption we are also very capable of finding very unique solutions to the problems that generally the world faces.

And one of them, of course, is the fact that we found freedom through non-violence and non-cooperation; who would've thought that was possible?

We have some other – no, seriously I mean it was as radical of thought then as it is today, and one man in a loincloth would believe in faith and complete conviction was able to do that for us — you know, Mahatma Gandhi, and it's an amazing country of people like Mahavir, Gautam Buddha and Mahatma Gandhi and then Bhagat Singh who also had a dream.

He dreamed then 85 years ago, that I dream of an India where no infant cries for the want of milk, no youngster is deprived of relevant education, and no youth goes door to door finding a job.

Sadly, it's still a dream today. And I dream of a 2030 when this dream becomes irrelevant.

I dream of a 2030 when everybody is so equally satisfied with what they're doing, that they're able to actually devote about more time back to art and culture which is another great important aspect of our country.

Now we need to be – for that to happen we need to be a healthy nation. And when I say healthy, I remember preparing for a film of mine which was released recently where I had to look like a boxer and I had this biceps and triceps that had to be there.

So I decided just to work on the parts that is seen outside my clothes. So I was just working out of my biceps and my triceps and my shoulders but you know what I suddenly realized, the strengths that I had in my arms and biceps was not actually enough for me to look even fit because it is disproportionate growth.

It is the kind of growth that will not make you fit or strong but actually make you look inadequate. And that is what is happening to India today.

Everybody says we are the largest economy — we're going to be the most populated country in the years to come and you know with economic superpower and supremacy in rocket and space technology which I am privy to and then the IT giants and smarter cities.

But ladies and gentlemen, I really believe that more than smarter cities we require smart villages. And this is going to be primarily what I talk about today.

You know, a nation is only as strong as its weakest link and rural India is our weakest link.

See, it's important that growth and progress goes hand-in-hand with villages also getting onto the same train towards economic freedom, super-powerdom, all terms that has been coined for a successful country but that is not happening, the reason being we're beginning to ignore them, we're beginning to actually believe that —

This is a very interesting line that I have found, where they say that everybody believes that they know what is required for getting the underprivileged and the poor up to speed with the rest of the country.

OK, and we always start assuming that this is what they want; this is how we can help the poor and the villages and this is what they need.

And we can't be more wrong, because when you assume, and as the spelling goes you make an ass of you and me, let me tell you how that happened to a friend of mine.

His name was — he's a very profound doctor, a gastroenterologist, and he got a call from his patient Mr. Abdul, who said, "Doctor Saab, my wife is really really ill and she's got a big stomach ache and she can't sit and she can't sleep and she's in big pain, can I come and visit you?"

And he said, 'Yes, by all means'.

And like all patients today he's done his research, he's gone into the internet and he said, "usko yeh ho sakta hain, wo sakta hain, and the doctor said, 'Don't worry let me handle it'.

And he checked her out and he said "She has an infected appendix, so I have to do a surgery and she'll be fine."

The surgery was done, she was fine and Abdul was a happy man.

One year later, he calls back to doctor and says, "Sir, my wife has got a stomach ache, please do the appendix operation, she'll be fine."

And so doctor said — the doctor Manu said,"Listen, I am the doctor, let me diagnose, Abdul, please bring her to the clinic and we'll fix it up."

But he said, 'No, no, sir fix up that operation date, we'll do it in half an hour and we'll be back — just she needs that appendix removed'.

So now he's losing his patience, he says "Let me do the diagnosis, Abdul, bring her to the clinic."

And he's still insisting and finally the doctor lost it, and he said, "Listen, I am the doctor and let me tell you that every
human being has only one appendix, and I have already taken out the appendix.

So please don't tell me how to do my job." Abdul waited very patiently for the doctor to finish with his assumptions and then he shot back very meekly, he says, "Sir, I agree with you, every human being can have one appendix but a man can have two wives, right?"

So when we start assuming what the rural India needs, we do what I think is most dangerous.

In my vast experiences of shooting in really rural India's, and villages and small [cook-gramins] like they call it in Tamil, really small places, I realized shockingly that the biggest financial burden for a person of this particular village, would you all be able to guess what his biggest financial burden is — five minutes!

Hey so I'm going to speak for 20 today, I am going to reduce the number of questions, I'm prepared, is that OK?

OK, so can you all tell me, anybody, quick answers — anybody know which is the biggest financial burden for a man in one of these small villages?

Sorry, tap, health, OK.

Not health, not the marriage of a daughter, not education, not – liquor, thank you for reminding me, no.

Say it again, dowry, no, no, no, no.

Let me put you out of your misery.

I'm saying why does he need financial assistance for — the answer is the untimely death of one relative of a senior in their family, that is the one occasion he can't prepare for, that is one occasion where the ceremony demands that he spend a certain amount of money, feed a certain amount of people, use the funeral expenditures and that's where he takes the loan and that's where he gets indebted and that's where, to escape that particular embarrassment and humility of not having the ability to perform the function every year as a specter of the Indian tradition that he decides to leave the village, because he's made to feel inadequate.

Lord Macaulay in 1735 had spoken in the British Parliament and said, "The only way to rule India is to make the men there feel inadequate",he said and truly so, that unless he feels that what he has is lesser than what others have, you will not be able to rule him.

And within a very short period they proved themselves right.

The rural India today is feeling inadequate, they are feeling like they're not even part of our country. And what happens with that is they start then looking at opportunities in villages and saying better education, better health, better lifestyle and no humility for not having performed the funeral properly, they decide to give up who they are and move to the cities. And who they are is what is more important for us to understand.

Who they are, are actually the timekeepers and the bookkeepers of our deep-rooted traditional culture and stories.

You know, you should see how tradition and culture flourishes in a happy village in India. We don't have psychiatrist as a big fashion thing in India and they still manage to maintain a great level of sanity.

You know, there's a great phrase from the poem, 'If' by Rudyard Kipling where it says, 'Dream but not make dreams your master; think but not make thoughts your aim; meet with triumph and disaster and treat those two Impostors just the same.'

It's very easy to say it but how do you treat those two Impostors just the same? The answer lies in the tradition and the culture and the books and the epics that are so prominent and predominant in our country – The Bhagavad Gita, the Koran, the interpretation of that in the subcontinent, the Bible, the Guru Granth Sahib, the Granny stories, and you know how to handle the diversities and the setbacks and you're able to sit back, assemble — reassemble yourself, come back and fight with the same glory again.

And we don't give him — when you don't give a villager that, you're depriving him, we're depriving ourselves of what I think is one of the most important survival tools in today's world, which is the culture and tradition.

So I dream of a 2030 where rural India is as developed as the rest of the world, is as aspirational as the rest of India and wher the villager is provided with the same opportunities as it is available in the cities. And after a hard day's work, a villager is actually able to come back, sit down, have a drink, put his feet up and start thinking about art and culture and poetry.

That would be a dream that I have for 2030 — a practical dream that I have for 2030.

And the dreams that your parents and my parents had when we were in college — urban middle class – where everything revolved around the boy, studying hard, getting into a technical college of a repute and then getting into a reputed managements college and finally the green card.

And if it was the girl, then it was a spouse with a green card.

I dream of a 2030 where students the world over will dream of a blue card, will dream of having once actually come to India and study and imbibe the knowledge that we have as a nation.

It used to be true: we were the first university in the world – Nalanda was the university where people came in from far and wide. So it's not a pipe dream, it's a practical dream that I have, and I think that's easily, easily attainable.

And finally, before I wind up, I think, I'll dream of a 2030 where we have a meritocratic electoral base which selects its leaders and whose leaders believe that it is more important to serve — with a missionary zeal to serve the nation rather than rule it.

You know, there is another stanza from the same poem which says that, if they have the ability to talk to the crowds yet keep your virtue, walk with Kings – nor lose the common touch, if neither good friends nor foes can hurt you, yet all men count with you but none too much — if only the politicians understood the gist of that line, we would have a progressive country by 2030 where we'll all be proud of not just the way the country is running but also proud about our politicians.

And finally, you know, I'm an actor and the dream that I have for myself is that in 2030 I'm as relevant and as handsome hopefully but if age was to catch up, then they probably would have mapped my face by then and use technology to make me look as young or old, as the role desired me to look, and I'm still able to romance the pretty young things that would be part of the industry in 2030. I see that's got many guys going ham.

And finally as an actor, I'm used and prone to dialogues, I love to speak dialogues, and I recently found a line that blew me apart and I thought it was a phenomenal Hindi film dialogue, where this great gentleman has said,"That whatever I am today and all the achievements that have been – that has been possible by me and what will eventually also be possible by me in the near future are all because of my angel mother."

Do you know who said that?

You know who said that?

Shockingly Abraham Lincoln!

So I dream of a 2030 where every Indian says the exact same thing about his mother and not just about his mother but also about his motherland – and also for the sake of posterity about his mother-in-law.

But hey, ladies and gentlemen, what do I know? I am an actor.

Thank you very much for your patient hearing.

www.ingramcontent.com/pod-product-compliance
Lightning Source LLC
Chambersburg PA
CBHW030645220526
45463CB00004B/1647